MOVING FORWARD

REYNAH GUPTA

Contents

Contents

Contents

Preface

This book came into being at midnight, possibly. The first few poems definitely did, muddled thoughts in February with too many emotions and a lot more fear than I have now. I wrote, constantly, for a few days and came up with way too many pages of crossed out words and haphazard thoughts that somehow twisted their way into a poem. I felt a lot as I wrote these poems, transferring myself onto the page.

That was the easy part. The harder part was realising what I felt everytime I wrote these poems in a haze, but I had the knowledge that I was not alone. In such a vast world, the knowledge that even though I feel insignificant, I am not alone and I never will be, is very precious to me. I put together my poems and wrote this so that I can help you remember that there are people who know exactly how you feel, and help is there everywhere, even if at one moment there's nothing in your mind but despair.

To be honest, the first few start with a lot of the negative side of life, the things that will not make you smile and made me feel a little sad when I read over them too. But through the poems I want to depict that things need to go down for them to go up, stars can't shine without darkness and that taking a break isn't a bad thing. It's called letting yourself heal, and everyone needs that.

Reynah Gupta.

1. Drowning

Some days
The darkness is my friend
And others
It is like water
And I have forgotten
That I know how to swim.
I have forgotten
That I have been here before
And that I am better now.
Most days,
I don't know what is left
But gasping breaths and
Watery eyes.

2. Middle Line Between Living and Not

How does one know
That they are living?
Is there a line
That one must cross
Between survival and living
To know what it is like to live?
If there is
Then I dance on the fine line
Too weak to last on one side
And too afraid of the other.

3. Ghosts

We are walking,
Our shadows on the walls and floor
Yet I am not completely
Sure
That we are not just
Ghosts
In this house
That should be home.

4. When Will You Realize I am Too Less

In my mind,

I dream and dream

Of the world ending

But I am always there when it does

And each time, you are there with me.

Fear catches me

And then I think,

Would I rather you be gone when I am at my weakest

Or would I rather only let you see me at my best?

Is it selfish to need help

And is it cruelty to hide away

Every little part of myself

That I can not bear

Am I ignoring myself

Just for you?

In my mind

I think there is an ending line,

Where I am too less

And you only love the image in your head.

5. The Chase

Run, girl, run
And she runs faster,
Burns on her feet
And scrapes on her knees.
He's gonna catch you
They say
And she screams and thinks
Of the last time,
Where burnt scorched feet felt like heaven
Compared to the cold licking
Her cheeks.
They speak words
And she runs faster
But the world will never let the runner
Win at tag if
There are no obstacles.
So the girl
Runs
Indefinitely,
Terrified and knowing
That a pile of bodies can not be her shield
And she will only ever know freedom with pain.

6. Laughter

I say I know
What is good for me,
But always,
As the day ends,
I look and think
Is there a light that can go out
If it was never there?
Can shadows exist
If there is nothing bright?
I stay on the middle line
Where laughter
Doesn't escape my throat
But my eyes
Don't burn with tears
Either.
There is as much tragedy in neutrality,
As there are liars in men.
I can say
I am one of them everytime
I say I do things that make me feel...

7. The Reaper

Is there a ghost I see
standing
Waiting for me?
Or is it the reaper,
Calculating how far I am from the ground,
Just to remember how many looked over the edge
And laughed as the wind,
Blew out the fire of the world?
Does the reaper see them
And wonder why some live
Because they wish to
And others see a hand that belongs to them
But is coated with only their own blood?
When he looks at those
With burning hearts that don't provide warmth
(not anymore),
Does he think them victims,
Or survivors,
Who learnt that surviving wasn't enough?
Does the reaper ever wonder,
Why death sends more to peace
Than it sends to grief?

8. Dreams

Don't dwell too much on the past
They say
But never remind us
That dwell on the future too much,
The world will crush you,
Dreams are weak,
Faint little ideas
Thought by the strongest too.
But they are not waif-like,
And each day one falls to their knees
Dreams sticking into them like knives.
Blood seeps out of open wounds,
And every failure,
Feels like one when dwelling on dreams
That are as far away as stars.
Coming close to them burns too.

9. Apathy

Grief was a friend,
Apathy was too.
And being a middleman,
Apathy was toxic,
But so, so convincing
The others wonder
Why words don't harm me,
And love doesn't heal me.
But when I had a choice,
I made one.
Whether it was wrong
Or right,
It was a choice I made,
And the world will try
To hurt,
But being shrouded by apathy
Is like a cage for grief
And has never tasted more sweet.

10. End

The sea comes as a tempest,
And does not care to mind the innocent
Those who don't deserve it.
The sea swallows the foolish ones
And gleams
With a coat of
Innocence
And beauty sharpened to an edge with the sun's rays.
Nature
Is all encompassing
And it takes
And takes
Until there is nothing more to have
So at the end of the day
Will it be so surprising to see who will
Have the last laugh?

11. Broken Dolls

I can not
Trust the words I speak
Because what if they come from my heart
Will they look at me and wonder
If broken dolls lie like I do
With a smile on my face
And blood on my teeth?

I think
That they will wonder
And know the moment
That I speak
That they were wrong
I am close to nothing
Too far from living
To be breaking.

The void,
An empty abyss
Can not be broken apart.
So I can not,
Either.

12. Fear

Nothing's new this time,
It clogs my throat
And pushes at my ribs
It might stab my stomach too.
It grasps my head and shakes it
Like it is trying
To shake all the thoughts
Out of my mind.
It works,
Sometimes,
And on those days
It pulls at my cheeks too
And forces my eyes open.
I remember this feeling
As accurately as I remember my shadow.
It makes me lose
Control
And some days,
It makes me beg,
But says in my mind
You have begged before,
What will make this time any different?

13. Hollow Screams

There is shouting

Inside or outside

My head.

It burns

The words engraved in my mind

And in my soul.

I remember

On the good days

And then the screaming starts

All

Over

Again.

Fear burns

And collapses like a dying star

The moment I remember

That I left,

The moment I remember that I ran,

The screaming dulls

And I laugh

Till I cry.

14. Does The Guilt Burn?

Is she happy today
Or is she uncaring now?
Do her words surprise them
Or horrify them
Till she laughs to make it all worse?
Do her screams run rampant
In your mind
As you remember the child
You could have saved
When you think of cowardice,
Do you think of saving yourself
Or do you think of little kids learning
The harsh reality
Of blood and bruises and how much
The world really cares about the word no?
Does guilt crawl in every crevice
Of your mind,
Till its venom leads you to the terrace?
If you have watched or harmed,
If you have ever taken
What shouldn't have been taken
I hope the guilt flays you alive.

15. Missing Poison

The mirror laughs in my face
And on some days I turn away
But on others
Tears pour down my cheek as I wonder
What I have done so wrong
To have everything escape my grasp.
I miss my home,
And my friends say it is like missing poison.
But I guess
When people are poisoned
They are at least cared for.
People do many things for love
And poisoning myself on purpose
Is not the worst thing I could do.

16. Sometimes At Night

Sometimes at night
I pray for the people who
Lost their will.
I pity them
And I don't think they're below me.
Life dealt them a dangerous hand
And their entire life
Was a gamble on whether or not
This time would be too much
Or whether they could force themselves
To go just one more day.

Sometimes at night
I hope that I will never
Lose again
But I know that dreaming
Is not something that I can do
Without lying to myself.
I think of all the broken kids
Who were crushed under the force of the world.

Sometimes at night
I wish for the world to be gentler
And to dim its flame
But everything is in precarious positions
And the kids who lose and the adults who are losing
Are just collateral to the world
That has never known how to
Show kindness without breaking.

Sometimes at night
I wonder if the world's way to show kindness
Is to break someone again
And again
Until they have achieved the best
Versions of themselves they will ever be.
It is cruel
And sometimes
It goes wrong and the world is too cruel
To use its rough calloused hands
To save just another life.

Sometimes at night
I pray for the kids
Who survived too much

MOVING FORWARD

And experienced too little kindness
In their lives,
And I hope that somewhere
They will smile again.
I wish that the world stops being
Mindlessly cruel
And then I wonder
If that is just an
Unreachable dream.

17. Trying To Be What I Wanted Others To Be

I think there are times
Where I look people in the eye
And they thank me
While I can not help but feel the heaviness
Of a tortured soul sitting on my shoulder.
I hate to think that people like me
Have to be the ones to save someone
When others could have
Done so much better.
It's a horrible thing
To learn that the kind aren't
Always righteous and brave.

18. The Pain Of Regret and Sorrow

Sometimes I think of the night I fell
And I remember where
All that hatred came from.
And I think that people forget
That laurel wreaths and gold
Don't fix a broken soul.
I think I'd love to love who I was before
I got the glory that I longed for.
I see your face in the shadows still
And I wonder
If I'm allowed a broken heart and a broken soul.
I look at my friends
And they're all in graves or confronted by the danger
That I put them in.
Can I call them my friends
If I was the one that caused this
Just because I wanted someone to know
That I wasn't just a coward
That I was strong and worth it
But I'm not anymore.

19. Missing Piece

Somedays I find it hard
To admit that something in me
That belonged to you long ago
Left the day
That I learnt who you really are.
Some days I think that part of me was always
Meant to belong to you
And that is why
When I walked the path
Of being left alone
I walked with a vital part of me gone
Looking for someone that was no longer there.

20. Bruises

What did I do wrong today?
She thinks
As if the marks
That paint her skin in colors of the rainbow
Are her
Fault.

21. Fighting To Lose

On the days where I can only stare
And curl up in my bed
I long for a purpose to fight
Ghosts that faded away long ago.
On those days
I create problems for myself
With the promise that if I fight again
I will finally take a step forward
Even if it is a tiny one
But I never seem to realise
That I'm moving backward instead
And that causing myself pain
Will never help me take a step towards
That light I always dream of.

22. Deserved, Not Deserve

23. To Live

We don't know
How living really feels like
Until we have felt
What it is like
To die.

24. Importance

It is hard to accept
That one day
I will not be there
And the words I have said
Are as unimportant
As words written in the sand
As the sea comes to take them away.

25. Promises Of You

Night comes and I hold you,
Day comes and you hold me,
But then,
You start holding yourself in the night
And suddenly,
This game of
Give and take,
Is not for you anymore.
You are better now,
But I can still feel your broken promise
In my chest like a dagger,
As though my heart had clung onto it.

26. The Wonders Of Being Loved

I want to feel the love
That the poems talk about
That create illustrations in my mind
And I want to feel the love
That I feel when I sit on my bed and dream
With vivid flashes of soft whispers
And the complete understanding
Between interlocked fingers and featherlight touches.

27. Euphoria

Smiling is hard
When you have felt something closer to euphoria.
Feeling joy in the little things
Is easier and harder
When you have felt stronger
Emotions before.

28. Who Are You Really?

When the world crumbles around you,
Do you let your tears soak in the sand
Or do you pick up the rubble
And take care of the ashes?
Are you the phoenix
Or are you the flame?
Are you ready to be anything at all?

29. Disappointment

I wonder if disappointment
Means something bad
Or does it mean that I have done something
Better before and I have potential
To improve?
It's intimidating all the same
To experience the thoughts of failure
As it stabs in your heart everyday
And disappointment is your only friend.

30. Eyes Filled With Rage

They always say that I have angry eyes
That glare and burn
Anyone who dares approach near.
But I have always thought
That I have sad eyes
That have just the tiniest hope left
To rekindle misery
Into rage.

31. No

For once,
I said 'no'
And the world
Blinked,
Like it never thought
That I would learn
To play the game
Too.

32. I Want To Stop Hurting

I would like to go
To a world
Where people don't hurt.
The root cause
Of hurt
Is pain itself.
I would like to go a world
Where people didn't hurt
So I wouldn't be hurt either.

33. These Ashes Are Yours

The world's job
Is to push and push
and push
Until there is nothing left
But ashes to
Rise from.

34. I Chose You

Somewhere in the breeze,

It become you and me and no one else,

Somewhere in the breeze there was no one

To trust

And I started losing you

And I didn't know why

Because there were moments where

My memories were like ash hidden under gravel

And the world screamed,

Like it knew what would happen.

Like the moments lost between

You and I

Were meaningful.

Somewhere,

The breeze had convinced me that it would all be okay

And that one day it would be you who longed for just one hug.

But what happens till then?

For how long does one suffer

Till they get that sweet ray of light,

That tastes of honey and blood?

Too many lost things do not make one find worth it

And I was not willing to risk you,

Because if history was going to hide the one thing
I thought about
All day
All night,
Then the rose petals and gold
Wouldn't convince me
That it was a choice I really needed to think about.
It wouldn't convince me
That you weren't worth every
Single thing
I have left behind.

35. Thoughts Of You

I wish to say
The way I think
But the words I know
Can't be written
So I think until i cannot
Because if there is one thing
I know I can do
It is think
And I do not need words
To think of every inch
Of you. Just you.

36. Hold On

I think

That some days

Running away

Is the only thing I look forward to.

Getting out is the only thing that matters

And perhaps

I don't hate it too much.

Everyone needs that little something

To hold on to.

37. It's Worth It all

It takes one tiny mistake
One tiny miscalculation
To be forgotten forever
To be thrown away to the side.
But walking that line
Where you don't reach far enough forward to
Make that mistake
Only means that you were too scared
To be someone in the first place.

38. To Be Thought Of

Missing me
Is different from cradling my ashes
It is different from achilles' rage
When he lost patroclus
And missing me
Is not as big as
Crumbling to the ground as though untethered
From reality.
I prefer one because I care
And I think of the other often
Because I would love to be loved.

39. Truly Loved

I think
I'm done being loved by people
Who do not truly know me.
Listen closely,
If someone doesn't know what makes you
Who you are
There are chances
That there is better love waiting for you
Somewhere else.

40. Crying Is Okay

Go ahead and cry
Because your emotions are more
Valuable
Than you think they are.
Every part of you
Holds you up
And never forget that.

41. For Me

I think that some days
I forget that I exist solely
For myself
And that I do not owe anybody
Anything.
You belong to yourself
And the only person who doesn't know that
Is you.

42. I Will Not Stop

The world is cracked
Broken in its own way
And I crawl,
Knees bleeding and bones broken
But I am moving still.
I have paid too much
Lost too much
Come too far
Walked too many steps
To stop now.
The world might be against me
Might be trying to trip me up
But I have not walked so far and so long
To forget that I have built up
My balance
For when the only thing I have in the world
Is myself,
And that is enough.
If it isn't,
I will make it enough.

43. I Fought Enough To Be Here, Don't Deny Me This

I think I've fought enough
And I think the world is covered with my tears
Enough.
I think I deserve more now
I have spent too much time rebuilding Rome
After it burnt around me
To be treated to scraps and half burnt joys.
I deserve more
But I am not sure I can fight for it.
My hands shake
My breath is heavy
And I want what I have fought years for.
I long for something I have given too much for
And I long to be deserving of something.

44. Still Standing

There are ants crawling up my spine
And shivers wrapping my whole body
But I have not bowed yet
To the life that shows no mercy.
My head is up
And my spine is steady
And my feet don't shake.
Standing up when life is pressing on you
Even if you have tears pouring down your cheeks
Is a greater bravery than you think.

45. Live

Live

For you.

Live

Because you have worked so hard.

And live

Because life is trying so hard

To make sure you don't.

46. Light

Isn't it funny
To look back and realise
That you lived?
I look back
And I wonder sometimes
If it was worth it.
And then I remind myself
That I lived.
I have scraped myself
And my mind isn't the same as it was before
But the light
That I could barely see before
Is mine to control now.
It's in my hands
And no one can take it from me ever again.

47. You're Stronger Than You Think

You are brave
And the wolf in you roars.
You may not be a lion
With nobility running in your veins
But circuses can not capture a wolf.
You have the strength
And the mind,
And the blood running in your veins
May not make you feel strong,
But the ability
To have walked the hill of life
Till here,
Means you have strength
Anyway.

48. Burning Bright

Bravery is my father
And fierceness is my mother,
While I burn with a fire of my own.
I am not weak
I have not been raised to be someone who falls
And does not get back up.
I am rage
And everything from my parents before me
And that is all I need.
You can not tell me
To burn out
Just because you are too dim a flame.

49. You Only Think You Can Break Me

You may think
That you can hurt me in a way
That I have never been hurt before
And while that may be true
I have gone through the tunnel
Of darkness
And spent too long in it
To break because of someone
Who's only purpose in life
Is to cause others pain.

50. I Look At Life

I look at life
And I think the true meaning was right in front of us
Laughing and wondering when we'd understand what was life
Knowing that searching for a meaning was useless
Because why do we go on rollercoasters
If not to feel the ups and downs and
The adrenaline in the journey?

I look at life
And wonder if it's trying to cradle us
In a gentle hug even though it hurt us
One too many times with too sharp turns
And too steep slopes for the adrenaline to ever feel worth it.

I look at life
And I hope that it understands that we all need those days
Where we can't feel anything but blank
In a way that's hard to tell anyone
Because the world is blank and the adrenaline
Is like tethering on the edge of the abyss

And the rollercoaster feels like it's about to fall
But not down the tracks.

I look at life
And I see the strength that it took
To even reach the point where I could understand
That living is worth the pain.

51. You Held Me Together

I think too much and my gaze
Is hard and distant.
But the days I see the people
Who I have held onto tightly,
Even in my lost state
The days I see the people
Who I have held onto
Like my only link to life,
Those days
I let the joy pour out of open wounds
Rather than sorrow
And I feel the skin stitch together
As the wounds close.
And the feeling doesn't cause pain
As long as I feel the true love
Emanating from every person
Who refused to leave me.

52. One Foot Ahead Of The Other (Moving Forward)

Most nights
I have to remind myself that the path behind me
May not have been as hard as the journey in front
But that I have crawled and hurt
Too much just to reach here
And it may not be the end
And I may still be clouded by darkness
But I built my resilience already
And I taught myself how to put one foot in front of the other.

About The Author

Reynah Gupta is a tenth grade student in The Shri Ram School Aravali, Gurgaon. She is extremely passionate about art and has been painting for ten years. Her passion for the Art society landed her the designation of the Art Society Secretary for the academic session 2024-25. Besides art she also has a flair for writing and won Gold in the Queen's Commonwealth Essay Writing Competition among the 34,000+ international participants. She also received the bronze award under the International Award for Young People (IAYP), which is a member of the Duke of Edinburgh's International Award Association.

The author can be contacted at reynah.gupta@gmail.com.

Reynah's artworks available @reys_artx on Instagram.